W9-CCM-868

SUPER SIMPLE
EARTH INVESTIGATIONS

SUPER SIMPLE
WEATHER
PROJECTS

Science Activities for
Future Meteorologists

JESSIE ALKIRE

CONSULTING EDITOR, DIANE CRAIG, M.A./READING SPECIALIST

Super Sandcastle

An Imprint of Abdo Publishing
abdopublishing.com

abdopublishing.com

Published by Abdo Publishing, a division of ABDO, PO Box 398166, Minneapolis, Minnesota 55439. Copyright © 2018 by Abdo Consulting Group, Inc. International copyrights reserved in all countries. No part of this book may be reproduced in any form without written permission from the publisher. Super SandCastle™ is a trademark and logo of Abdo Publishing.

Printed in the United States of America, North Mankato, Minnesota
102017
012018

THIS BOOK CONTAINS RECYCLED MATERIALS

Design: Kelly Doudna, Mighty Media, Inc.
Production: Mighty Media, Inc.
Editor: Liz Salzmann
Cover Photographs: Mighty Media, Inc.; Shutterstock
Interior Photographs: AP Images; Mighty Media, Inc.; Shutterstock; Wikimedia Commons

The following manufacturers/names appearing in this book are trademarks: Aleene's® Original Tacky Glue®, Dawn®, Durasharp®, Elmer's® Glue-All®, Equaline®, Gedney®, Pyrex®, Sharpie®, Stanley® Bostitch®, Westcott®

Publisher's Cataloging-in-Publication Data
Names: Alkire, Jessie, author.
Title: Super simple weather projects: science activities for future meteorologists / by Jessie Alkire.
Other titles: Science activities for future meteorologists
Description: Minneapolis, Minnesota : Abdo Publishing, 2018. | Series: Super simple earth investigations
Identifiers: LCCN 2017946521 | ISBN 9781532112416 (lib.bdg.) | ISBN 9781614799832 (ebook)
Subjects: LCSH: Meteorology--Juvenile literature. | Weather forecasting--Juvenile literature. | Science--Experiments--Juvenile literature.
Classification: DDC 507.8--dc23
LC record available at https://lccn.loc.gov/2017946521

Super SandCastle™ books are created by a team of professional educators, reading specialists, and content developers around five essential components—phonemic awareness, phonics, vocabulary, text comprehension, and fluency—to assist young readers as they develop reading skills and strategies and increase their general knowledge. All books are written, reviewed, and leveled for guided reading and early reading intervention programs for use in shared, guided, and independent reading and writing activities to support a balanced approach to literacy instruction.

TO ADULT HELPERS

The projects in this title are fun and simple. There are just a few things to remember. Kids may be using messy materials such as glue or paint. Make sure they protect their clothes and work surfaces. Review the projects before starting, and be ready to assist when necessary.

CONTENTS

WHAT ARE WEATHER AND CLIMATE?

Weather is the condition of the atmosphere at one time and place. This includes temperature and wind speed. Weather is also sunny, cloudy, or rainy.

Storms, such as **tornadoes**, blizzards, and **hurricanes** are also part of the weather. Storms are sometimes called **extreme** weather. Other kinds of extreme weather include floods and **droughts**.

HURRICANE

FLOODED AREAS

SOME COASTAL AREAS THAT WOULD BE FLOODED
IF THE SEA LEVEL ROSE 1 FOOT (0.3 M)

Climate is the average weather over many years. Climate changes slowly. It can take thousands of years for climate to change.

Earth's climate is currently changing. It is slowly getting warmer. Even small changes in Earth's temperature can have large effects.

Warmer temperatures melt ice. This is harmful to animals such as polar bears. Melting ice can also cause sea levels to rise. This could flood islands and coastal cities.

POLAR BEAR MOTHER AND CUBS

CAUSES OF WEATHER

Weather is mainly caused by the sun. The sun doesn't heat Earth evenly. This is because of Earth's round shape. Uneven heating causes different temperatures in different places.

Weather is also affected by air pressure and movement. Uneven heating causes areas of different air pressures. Clear skies are caused by high pressure. Cloudy skies are caused by low pressure. Air moves to even out the air pressure. This is what causes wind!

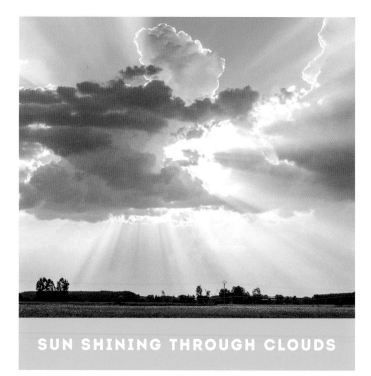

SUN SHINING THROUGH CLOUDS

SPRING   **SUMMER**   **FALL**   **WINTER**

Weather changes during seasons are caused by Earth's tilt and orbit. Earth moves around the sun. This takes 365.25 days.

As Earth moves, different parts of the planet receive sunlight more directly. The area tilted toward the sun has summer weather. The area tilted away from the sun has winter weather.

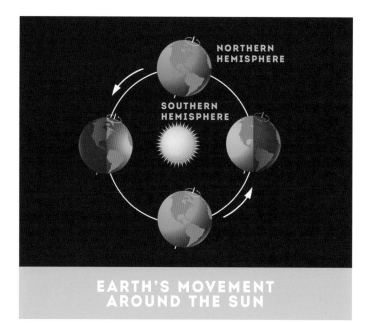

EARTH'S MOVEMENT AROUND THE SUN

HOW SCIENTISTS STUDY WEATHER

Some scientists study weather. They are called meteorologists. They **predict** weather. This helps people stay safe in storms.

Meteorologists work in weather stations around the world. Many meteorologists make weather forecasts. Forecasts include temperature, cloud cover, and storms. Forecasts can be for days, weeks, or even months ahead.

Meteorologists use tools to study and predict weather. These include thermometers, anemometers, and barometers. Scientists also use **satellites** and **radar** to create computer forecast models.

WEATHER SATELLITE DISHES

JOHN DALTON

John Dalton was an early meteorologist. He was born in England in 1766. Dalton kept daily weather records for more than 50 years. He measured temperature, **precipitation**, wind speed, and air pressure. Dalton published a book about meteorology in 1793. Many call Dalton a father of meteorology!

METEOROLOGIST TRACKING A STORM

Some meteorologists study climate. They study long-term changes and patterns. They learn what causes climate change. They look for ways we can slow or prevent these changes.

MATERIALS

Here are some of the materials that you will need for the projects in this book.

BALLOON

CARD STOCK

CLEAR GLASS
CONTAINER

COTTON BALLS

CRAFT GLUE

DISH SOAP

EYEDROPPER

FOOD COLORING

GLASS JAR

GLITTER

HAIR ELASTIC

HOLE PUNCH

LARGE ROUND PLASTIC LID

MARKERS

MEASURING SPOONS

PAINT PENS

PENCIL WITH ERASER

PLASTIC DRINKING STRAWS

PUSHPINS

SHAVING CREAM

SMALL PAPER CUPS

SMALL PLASTIC CUPS

STAPLER

VINEGAR

TIPS AND TECHNIQUES

Set up your own weather station! Use a thermometer, barometer, and anemometer to track different weather measurements. Also, you can find electronic weather stations for sale **online** and at **hardware** stores.

WATER CYCLE MODEL

MATERIALS: large round plastic lid, card stock (various colors), markers, scissors, ruler, white paint pen, stapler, tape, hole punch, string

Water moves in a cycle. It changes from solid to liquid to gas over and over. This causes **precipitation**, such as rain and snow.

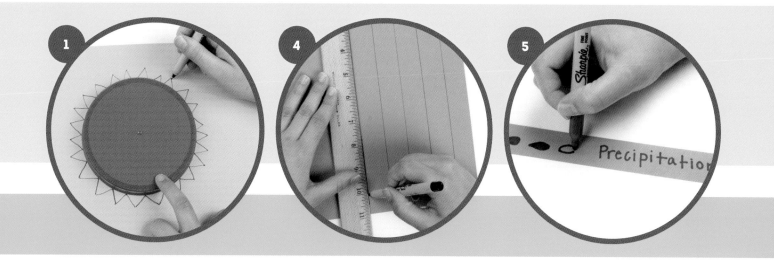

1 Place the lid on a sheet of card stock. Draw triangles around the lid to make a sun shape.

2 Cut the sun out.

3 Cut a strip out of dark blue card stock. Make it 1½ by 11½ inches (4 by 30 cm). Repeat with white card stock.

4 Use a ruler to draw five straight lines on light blue card stock. Draw them 1 inch (2.5 cm) apart. Cut on the lines to create five strips.

5 Use a blue marker to draw raindrops on three of the light blue strips. Write "**precipitation**" on these strips.

6 Use a white paint pen to draw raindrops on the other two light blue strips. Write "**evaporation**" on these strips.

7 Use a gray marker to draw clouds on the white strip. Write "**condensation**" on this strip.

Continued on the next page.

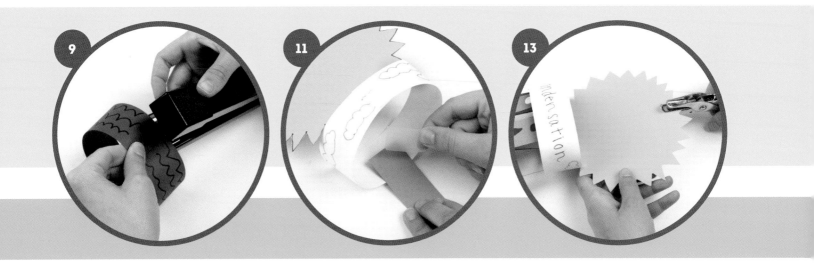

8 Use a black marker to draw waves on the dark blue strip. Write "collection" on this strip.

9 Staple the ends of the dark blue strip together so it forms a ring. Repeat with the white strip.

10 Tape the sun to the inside of the white ring.

11 Tape one end of each light blue strip to the inside of the white ring. Space the strips apart evenly.

12 Tape the opposite ends of the light blue strips to the inside of the dark blue ring.

13 Punch a hole in the top of the sun.

14 Tie a string through the hole. Use the string to hang up your water cycle wherever you'd like!

DIGGING DEEPER

In the water cycle, water changes its form over and over. The sun heats bodies of water. Some of the water **evaporates** into a gas. The gas rises into the air. It cools and **condenses** into clouds. Then the water falls from clouds as **precipitation**. Types of precipitation include rain, hail, and snow. Precipitation collects on the ground and in bodies of water. The water evaporates again, and the cycle repeats.

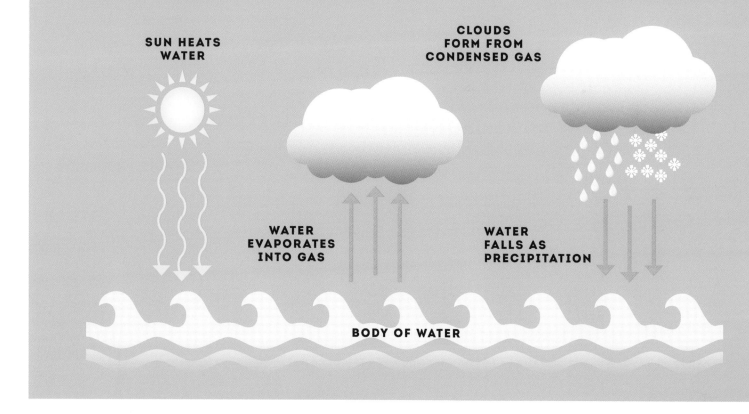

SUN HEATS
WATER

CLOUDS
FORM FROM
CONDENSED GAS

WATER
EVAPORATES
INTO GAS

WATER
FALLS AS
PRECIPITATION

BODY OF WATER

FLUFFY CLOUD POSTER

MATERIALS: blue card stock, cotton balls, craft glue, marker, paper, scissors, tape

Clouds are made of water drops or ice crystals. There are many kinds of clouds. Clouds are named by their shape and location in the sky. A cumulus cloud is white, thick, and puffy. A stratus cloud is a low cloud that stretches over a large area. A cirrus cloud is a high, thin, white cloud of tiny ice crystals. A cumulonimbus cloud is a large, low, dark cloud that often produces a storm.

Cumulus

Stratus

Cirrus

Cumulonimbus

1. Fold the card stock in half crosswise. Unfold it.

2. Slightly stretch four cotton balls. Glue them in one corner of the card stock. These are cumulus clouds.

3. Stretch a cotton ball until it is flat and wispy. Glue it in another corner. This is a stratus cloud.

4. Pull several small pieces off a cotton ball. Stretch them until they are very thin. Glue them in the third corner. These are cirrus clouds.

5. Slightly stretch five cotton balls. Color them with gray or black marker. Glue them together in a large clump in the fourth corner. This is a cumulonimbus cloud!

6. Make paper labels for the clouds. Tape the labels to the card stock.

JAR BAROMETER

MATERIALS: balloon, scissors, glass jar, hair elastic, plastic drinking straw, tape, ruler, card stock, markers

Meteorologists use barometers. These devices measure air pressure. Air pressure is the weight of the atmosphere. Changes in pressure can mean rain or storms are coming!

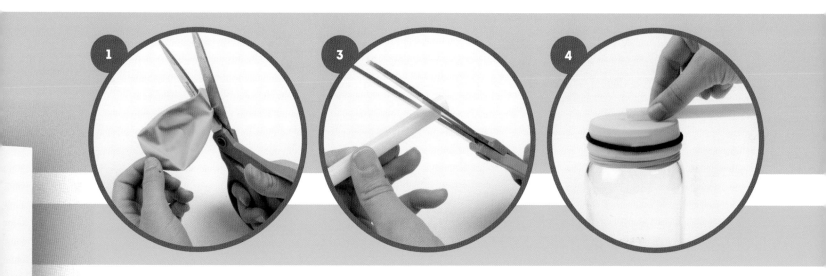

1 Cut the neck off the balloon.

2 Stretch the balloon over the top of the jar until it fits tightly. Secure the balloon with a hair elastic.

3 Cut one end of the straw at an angle to create a pointer.

4 Tape the uncut end of the straw to the center of the balloon.

5 Cut a piece of card stock that is about 4 inches (10 cm) taller than the jar.

Continued on the next page.

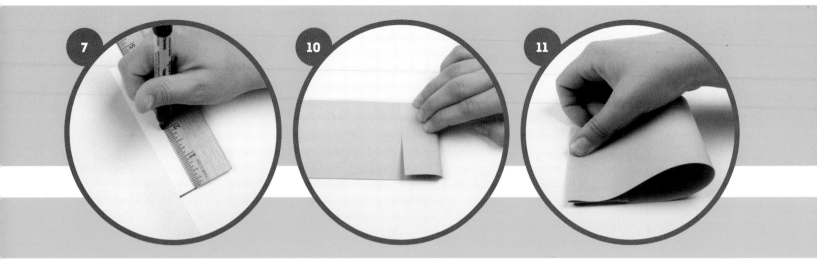

⑥ Hold the card stock next to the jar. Draw a line on the card stock where the straw points to.

7 Draw a line 2 inches (5 cm) above the first line. Draw a sun next to this line.

8 Draw a line 2 inches (5 cm) below the first line. Draw raindrops next to this line. This piece of card stock is the barometer's scale.

⑨ Cut a strip of card stock that is 3 by 11½ inches (7.5 by 30 cm).

10 Fold each end of the strip in 1 inch (2.5 cm).

11 Fold the strip in half.

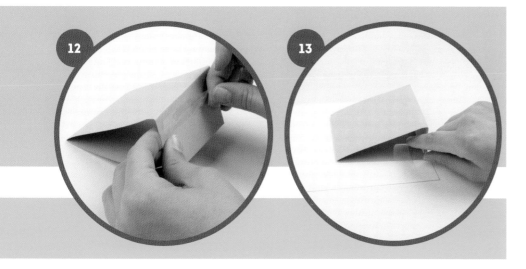

12 Open the end folds and tape them together so the strip forms a triangle. This is the stand for the barometer's scale.

13 Place the barometer's scale facedown. Lay the stand on top. Line the bottom up with the bottom of the scale. Tape the stand in place.

14 Place the jar near a window. Set the scale next to the jar. Make sure the pointer reaches across the edge of the scale.

15 Observe the straw and watch how much it moves due to changes in air pressure! Does it match the weather outside?

DIGGING DEEPER

Measuring air pressure with a barometer is one way to **predict** the weather.

High air pressure makes it hard for clouds to form. So it is likely to be sunny.

Low air pressure lets clouds form more easily. So it is more likely to rain.

In this project, air pressure affects the balloon. High pressure causes the balloon to be sucked into the jar. This pushes the end of the pointer up on the scale.

Low pressure causes the balloon to puff up. This pushes the pointer down on the scale.

SHAVING CREAM RAIN CLOUDS

MATERIALS: small plastic cups, water, food coloring, clear glass container, shaving cream, eyedropper

Clouds are made from water droplets. Sometimes the droplets fall. This is one form of **precipitation**!

1 Fill several small cups about halfway with water. Add drops of food coloring.

2 Fill a large glass container three-fourths full with water.

3 Spray shaving cream clouds on top of the water.

4 Use an eyedropper to drip colored water on the clouds. The water makes the shaving cream clouds heavier. Soon it causes rain to fall!

5 Add water faster by pouring it slowly out of a cup. How does the rainfall change?

SPARKLY TORNADO

MATERIALS: clear jar with lid, water, measuring spoons, dish soap, vinegar, glitter

Sometimes **tornadoes** occur. Tornadoes are narrow columns of air. They can spin at high speeds and cause a lot of harm.

① Fill the jar three-fourths full of water.

② Add a teaspoon of dish soap and a teaspoon of vinegar to the water.

③ Add glitter to the water.

④ Put the lid on the jar. Make sure it's sealed tightly!

⑤ Swirl the jar in a circular motion to see your **tornado** spin! Try different speeds and directions and observe how the tornado changes.

SPINNING ANEMOMETER

MATERIALS: 5 small paper cups, hole punch, pencil with eraser, 2 plastic drinking straws, stapler, pushpin, marker, electric fan (optional), timer, pen, notebook

Meteorologists use anemometers to measure wind speed. These tools help meteorologists track current weather conditions. They also help meteorologists make forecasts.

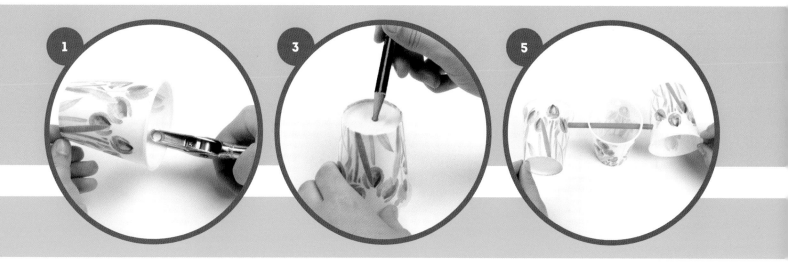

1 Punch four evenly spaced holes in one paper cup. The holes should be just below the rim of the cup. This will be the center cup.

2 Punch one hole in each of the other four paper cups. The holes should be about 1 inch (2.5 cm) below the rims of the cups. These will be the outer cups.

3 Use a pencil to poke a hole in the bottom of the center cup.

4 Push a straw through two opposite holes in the center cup.

5 Stick the ends of the straw through the holes in two of the outer cups.

Continued on the next page.

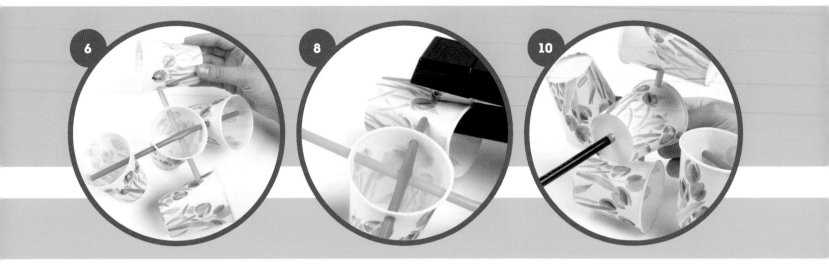

⑥ Repeat steps 4 and 5 with the remaining straw and outer cups.

⑦ Turn the outer cups sideways so they all face the same direction.

⑧ Staple the ends of the straws to the outer cups.

⑨ Stick a pushpin through the straws where they cross.

⑩ Push the eraser end of the pencil up through the hole in the center cup.

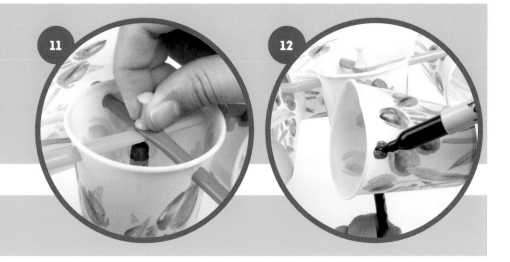

11 Stick the pushpin into the eraser.

12 Make a mark on the outside of one of the outer cups.

13 Take your anemometer outside on a windy day. Or, hold the anemometer in front of a powerful fan.

14 Use a timer to see how many times the anemometer rotates in one minute. Each time the marked cup goes by is one rotation. Write the number of rotations down.

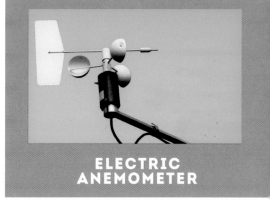

CONCLUSION

Weather is the state of the atmosphere at one place and time. Climate is the average weather over many years. Meteorologists study weather and climate. They make forecasts and help people plan!

QUIZ

1. Earth's climate is slowly getting colder.
   TRUE OR FALSE?

2. What causes seasons?

3. What do barometers measure?

LEARN MORE ABOUT IT!

You can find out more about weather and climate at the library. Or you can ask an adult to help you **research** weather and climate **online**!

Answers: 1. False   2. Earth's tilt and orbit   3. Air pressure

GLOSSARY

condense – to change from a gas into a liquid or a solid. This process is condensation.

drought – a long period of dry weather.

evaporate – to change from a liquid into a gas. This process is evaporation.

extreme – very much, or to a very great degree.

hardware – tools and supplies used to build things.

hurricane – a tropical storm with very high winds that starts in the ocean and moves toward land.

online – connected to the Internet.

precipitation – water that falls from the sky as hail, mist, rain, sleet, or snow.

predict – to say what will happen in the future.

radar – an instrument that uses the reflection of radio waves to detect and track objects.

research – to find out more about something.

satellite – a human-made object that orbits Earth. Satellites can send scientific information to Earth.

tornado – a violent whirling wind accompanied by a funnel-shaped cloud that moves along the ground in a narrow path.